There are
Animals
in my
Alphabet

written and illustrated
by Pat Houlihan
ISBN#979-8-9905215-0-6
Tanta Fairy Books, Publisher

A is for Alpaca

Alpacas are smart and gentle.

Alpacas live at high Altitudes in South America.

Alpacas only have bottom teeth.

Alpacas long curly hair is used to make sweaters and socks.

B is for Beaver

Beavers are Big Busy Builders.

They Build Beefy dams to Block water from flowing into their homes

By Biting through tree Branches using their orange, iron coated front teeth.

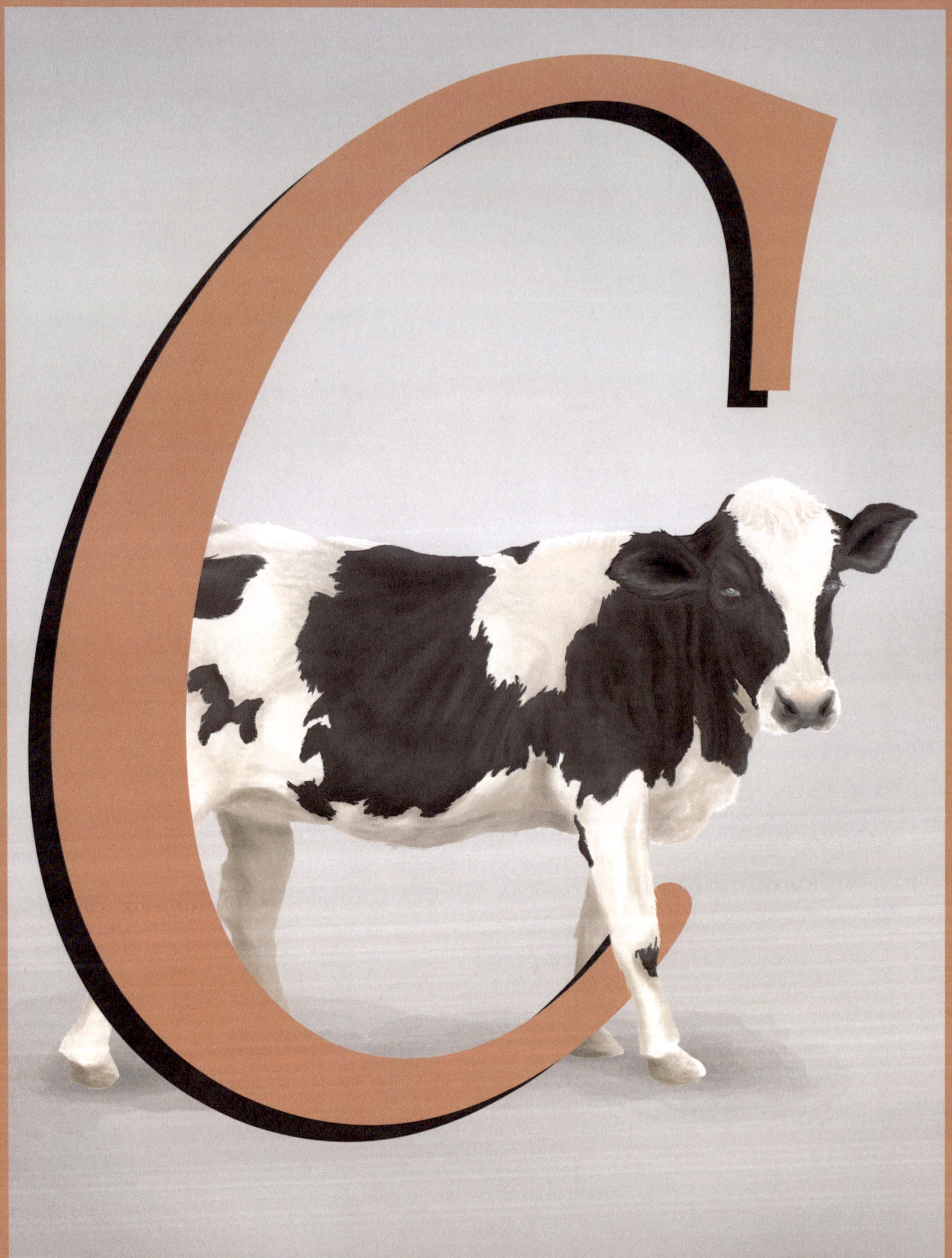

C is for Cow

Cows are one of the most Common farm animals in the world.

Baby Cows are Called "Calves."

While Cows usually spend around 10 hours a day lying Contentedly in the field, they only actually sleep about 30 minutes a day.

Cows have a strong sense of smell. They Can smell up to 6 miles away, so don't bother trying to Creep up on one!

D is for Duck

A baby Duck is called a "Duckling"

Ducks have a Double layer of feathers to keep them waterproof. The inside layer of feathers is called "Down".

Ducks sleep with half their brain awake. The outer circle of a sleeping flock, sleeps with one eye open to be alert to predators.

E is for Elephant

Herds of Elephants are called "matriachies" with the Eldest female as the leader.

An African Elephant's Ears are shaped like the African Continent.

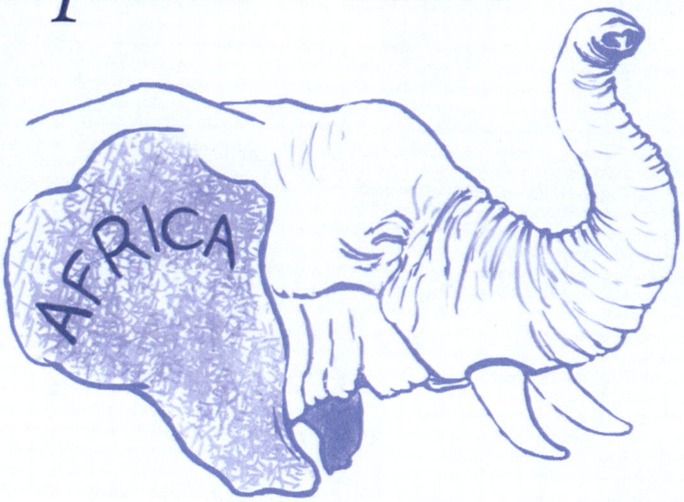

An Elephant's feet can "hear" or sense another Elephant's rumble from miles away.

F is for Fox

Foxes are Friendly and curious.

A Fox Family is called a "leash" or a "skulk" and they live in a hole in the ground called a "burrow".

They are the only member of the dog Family that can climb trees.

oh...and the Fox has a big Furry tail!

G is for Giraffe

Giraffes are Genial and
Good-natured.

They live on the plains of the African
Savannah, Gathered in Giraffe herds,
amongst other animals.

Giraffes have Giant necks allowing
them to eat from tree tops.

Because they are so tall they can Gaze
far across the plains and provide early
warning to other animals when danger
is approaching.

H is for Hippopotamus

Hippos are Heavy Herbivores.

Hippos can be Heard Honking to each other to communicate.

While too Hefty to swim, Hippos love to stand in the water to avoid the Heat of the day.

So do Humans, I suppose!

I is for *I*mpala

*I*mpalas are slender, fast and
agile.

*I*mpalas are *I*ndigenous to
Africa.

They can leap *I*ncredibly high and
far.

For protection they travel

*I*n herds.

I is for Jaguar

Jaguars are the most Jumbo of cats in the Americas.

Like leopards, Jaguars are Jam packed

with spots, but a Jaguar's spots usually have spots inside their spots.

They are excellent swimmers.

K is for Kangaroo

Kangaroos are strong,

Keen jumpers.

Their Kids are called "joeys" and ride in their mothers' front pouch.

Their tails are so strong that Kangaroos can balance their whole body upon them.

L is for Loris

Loris' Live in rainforests.

They Like eating bugs and fruits and Leaves.

The Loris has really Large eyes that help them see Long distances and see Late at night when there is Little Light.

M is for Moose

A Male Moose has Massive antlers that can Measure up to 6 feet across.

Moose are graceful on land and in water. They can run up to 35 Miles per hour.

Moose like to Meander in solitude in a Meadow or forest.

N is for Newt

Newts like to Nourish themselves with slugs and worms and insects.

If Newts lose an arm or leg they are able to grow New ones.

Many Newt species have poison glands in their skin to protect them from predators.

O is for Okapi

Okapis are the Only relative of the giraffe.

Okapis are shy and solitary. They are rarely seen in the wild.

An Okapi's tongue is so long that it can clean it's eyes and ears with it.

P is for Porcupine

Porcupines have Pointy spear like quills or hair to Protect them from Predators.

A group of Porcupines is called a "Prickle".

Baby Porcupines are called "Porcupettes".

Q is for Quokka

Quokkas are known as the "world's happiest animals" for their Quirky smiles.

Quokkas can only be found in Rottnest Island or Bald Island in Australia.

Originally thought to be Quite large rats, Quokkas are actually in the kangaroo family, with pouches for carrying their kids.

R is for Racoon

Racoons have a very high IQ and are known to clean their food in a River before eating.

Both a Racoon's front and Rear paws Resemble a human hand with 5 fingers or toes.

Racoons are not social animals. They might look cuddly but can be fearsome if approached, so
BEWARE!

S is for Squirrel

A group of Squirrels is called a
"Scurry."

Baby Squirrels, called "kits", cannot
See for the first 6 weeks of life.

Squirrels can fall from up to 100 feet
without hurting themselves.

A Squirrel's front teeth never Stop
growing, So they continuously
Snack on nuts to keep them filed
down.

T is for Tiger

A Tiger is the largest cat species in the world.

You can hear the Tiger's Terrific roar up to Two miles away!

No Two Tiger's have the same stripe pattern. Each pattern is Totally unique.

U is for Urial

A male Urial , also known as a ram, has very large curly "c" shaped horns.

Urials like to socialize with each other, so travel in large flocks.

The male Urial Uses his horns to fight other males. The Ultimate winner is the leader of the flock.

V is for *Vulture*

The King *V*ulture is a
*V*ibrantly colored, *V*oracious scavenger.

A group of resting *V*ultures is called
a "committee", or "*V*olt".

From high in the sky, they use their excellent
*V*ision to scan over a large area of ground
in search of carrion.

W is for Walrus

Walrus' can Weigh over 3,000 pounds!

The name Walrus means "tooth-Walking sea horse" in latin.

Walrus' have long tusks that are used to help haul themselves out of the Water and onto the ice.

X is for Xarnofal

The Xarnofal is considered to be regal among all animals. They are stronger than 20 humans combined, yet gentle in nature. Their massive wings allow them to soar to great heights and travel long distances. Known as a "protector", it is said, when in harms way, the Xarnofal has lifted and carried other animals to safety. While a mysteriously silent and elusive creature, if you close your eyes tightly enough, you will find the Xarnofal deep in the rainforest of your imagination.

Y is for Yak

Yaks are often used as pack animals. They are sure footed in the mountains and can carry up to 150 pounds!

You might notice, Yaks have two layers of fur to insulate them from the sub zero weather in the mountains.

In Tibet, Yak butter and milk are used to make butter tea called "po cha."

Z is for Zebra

Zebras are courageous animals with a Zingy kick.

They are one of few animals that can see in color.

Zebras can Zoom at speeds up to 65 mph.

Zebras sleep standing up.

Besides the Zoo, Zebras are found in Africa.